Insolence

Insolence

AND OTHER POEMS

Arya Shukla

AMARYLLIS

AMARYLLIS
An imprint of Manjul Publishing House Pvt. Ltd.
• C-16, Sector 3, Noida, Uttar Pradesh 201301, India
Website: www.manjulindia.com
Registered Office:
• 2nd Floor, Usha Preet Complex, 42 Malviya Nagar, Bhopal 462 003 – India
Distribution Centres
Ahmedabad, Bengaluru, Bhopal, Chennai, Hyderabad,
Kolkata, Mumbai, Noida, Pune

Insolence and Other Poems by Arya Shukla

This hardcover edition first published in India in 2024

ISBN 978-93-5543-509-5

Cover design: Trinankur Banerjee

Printed and bound in India by Parksons Graphics Pvt. Ltd.

To Kalyani, the very best of human existence.
I am privileged to bask in your light. All my love.

Contents

*The book contains discussions of mental health, self harm and disordered eating.

Creature of the Ash

You lived a fermented youth, feral and fertile
The kind of stuff that is whispered about in the
Jungle of souls and trees and concrete buildings
Did I envy it, the past of yours that you lived in?
So venomously, with such passion that I blush

At the thought of doing the same, I am but
A mourning creature of the ash, wounded and
Window-less suffocating in my own flesh, watching
As it grows looser and begins to stench the curtains
I do not have the upholstery of your youth.

I am a taint on the kind of child you wished you
Could have had; wishing is futile and you bore
Fruit to the truly mundane one; so wrapped up
In my own sorrow and morbidity that I forget
My sadness is not unique, everyone is sad and bad.

Just like you were, but I am not the outlier you were
I do not possess the same animal of ash that you
Held dear to your person, I am perpetually flailing
Against the boiling waters you threw me in, steaming
Into a soup of misery, a deluxe kind of misery that unlatches

From our bodies and mixes into our breath, that burdens
Your shoulders with the weight of proving you are
Still great despite me, mother. I am not wild and
With waving hair the way you were, I have shorn my head
And dismantled the womanly in me.

Forever Is Only Valid the First Time You Said It

You promise for eternity in this sea of uncertain tiptoes
Movements of the divine eternal flame catch your eye
And once again you forget to answer the quiz you made

- Am I taller than her?
- Does she make more than me?
- Will her soul carve mine up when she ends it this time?
- Can my ancestors forgive me for the things I have to do?
- Who do I answer to when I leave this world?
- Will my body just be ash floating in the water?

Time latches onto you like a lie you told your sixth-grade teacher it becomes your telling tick, the sign you have for when hope is too hard to hold on to and your hands have always been sweaty.

Afternoon Tea

We make afternoon tea from the second batch
of tea leaves we started our morning with.
The first batch went to the compost bin,
but the second we strain over in the sieve and leave
lidded over the saucepan, waiting
for the clock to strike three, when your lunch
nap has been consumed with half a rusk.
Then it is time for some slightly bitter tea
it curls into the buds of our tongues, solidifying.
But then there is sugar or jaggery for the weight
that rushes over those burns of pithy bitterness
like a wave shorn from the sea, hitting high rocks.
I am waiting for your nod of approval, and then I slump.
You claw at your cup like the burning hot tea will
wake you from the nightmares of the day and the night,
like it will unclench your flesh from bones
and present it as a slightly stale offering
beside the too-dry rusk and the bubbling tea,
there is a sign behind you,
right over the left corner of your too-flat head that reads –

confine me before it gets bad

our conversations are vague platitudes
of the day we have both been having,

drifting cubicles in seas of solitude,
what welcome solitude.
You make a list on your head and neck
and arms about what you wish people said to you,
and what people did say to you. Of things you wish
your mother had decided and your father had not,
it reads garishly like texts from a boy you broke
up with in the tenth grade and then dated again
in the summer between first and second year of uni.

- I am become a force to reckon myself with.
- I am whatever you want me to be.
- If you take me back now, I will forgive you.

And some don't read like titles of vaguely threatening emails,
they read like a plea or an epiphany you have in the wings
of the auditorium right before you go on stage to perform the
loudest song you don't know how to sing and
if you did, I would watch you in raptured awe,
waiting to yell and shout and cheer for the list
you have wrapped around your body.
We don't talk about it, but you mumble words from the list
out to me, sometimes amidst the other conversations we have
over tea.

- What type of coffee is a source of plant?
- The sun could eat us all and I would let it.
- Sometimes I see strangers and wonder if they are

happy, truly happy from their stomachs and not just their cheeks.

- I am ravenous and this tea is not enough.
- I am overfull and this tea will burst me open.
- I am am am am am, and I am not, I wish I was not, I do not want to be.
- I was made a host of my own body pushing it into display for others. Love is forsaken by bodies like mine and so I have stopped trying.
- I call out to my aunt who is pretty, she has always been pretty, someday she will be old and I look at her – named Doll at sixty and wonder if it was worth anything in the end.

In the end, always at the last sip of your tea,
where the drain of our sieve has leaked a few leaves into
the cup, this sip which I always pass and you gulp down,
you tell me – we should use fresh leaves.

Tasty

Your love is a thing that I could,
Fill my empty stomach with.
Like persimmons, ripe from the air of the season
Just waiting to be bitten into, teeth pulling
on flesh, until the skin breaks, a little at first
and juice gushes out into my mouth.
I am finally content, but I will never
Be full, like a beast.
A beautiful beast in love.

Breaking Your Mirror: Reported Health Benefits

On this ritualistic morning, I check the news,
murder, theft, murder, bus burning, fraud.

Refreshing with tea, steeped just right, boiled with milk and cardamom pods.

I then polish our shoes, a habit I haven't lost from my school days.
Squat on the last stair step like a dilapidated home, hunched over,
I am Quasimodo, but I didn't burn anything down this time.

Over on the news, information is shattered atop my head,
like bulbs of filament, a few pieces filter through into
my mind and I sit with swirls of data I know nothing more about.

Responsibility dictates I educate myself further,
but I am numb, here – check for yourself,
poke me with this pin and I don't even flinch anymore.

Creature of routine, because the smallest detour
will shatter any illusion of normalcy I have created.

The world is on fire, when will I stop to smell the smoke?

Free-falling Dreamscape

In my dream, I rule seven kingdoms, at least.
They are wild and unyielding,
chaos is the language and mayhem the stage,
of my dreams and my kingdoms.
There are five centipedes who look like seahorses,
They captain the army – water and land forces.
These seahorse-centipedes, they hate me. I am a bad queen,
With no rules – except that centipedes cannot be seahorses.

In my dream, the dinosaurs come for tea parties.
They wear pretty sarees
and they don't complain
about how much masala Ma puts in the chai.
Maybe they too slipped into a rabbit hole, is this wonderland?
Everything is late here,
the chai, the guests; the dinosaurs who we drank up –
They vanish; as though the earth split up and ate them.
Then we sucked them out, like that glucose ad,
where the sun sucks out energy with a straw.
But in my dream, the dinosaurs are pretty,
their scales shine against the sun.

My dream is late too. I take time to fall,
But then I do, earth open, body propelling
at so many miles an hour, that when I land

Morning has come and my body aches on the asphalt.
Concrete in my bones, I sag to the admissions counter.
I am late, the cut-offs are out and I cannot find my name.
Did I make it, tick tick tick, did I slip, foot on water
Friction-free, I fall and
the throne is there – so I sit up and open my eyes.

Fumes of Fire

I gulp down fumes of purple
Burnished magenta hues, bright, so
Bright
Like broken thuds
Of the drums I sat in,
And they kept beating,
to tunes I felt in my bones,
until my bones were
mixed
With the dust of our ancestors.
Would they envy these purple fumes,
That envelop as I laugh without
Cadence
Or
Care
Or
Consideration
For the others, outside my body?

Holidays For You and Me

Holidays are for invisible ghosts
that slither down from the cobwebs in the house.
They creep out, wandering in the emptiness
of four walls with prior claim,
Frauds, but they may be deeper than you and I,
we ran away to Shimla in the winters.
Would the ghost in our house let settle
our perfect crystal, or will it thaw all the same.
Holidays are for the ghoul in our house,
they split out from our anger renounced
And together they pace the house like
tiny little freaks of green emotion.

They circle the kitchen, where you don't
clean the counter and I make terrible chai,
But we're on a holiday and we have snow,
we buy our chai; the counter is not ours to clean.
So the ghoul and the ghost take over our house.
They shed their dust and flex their mean
Muscles, while we breathe in cleaner air,
brush settlements of the house a brief goodbye.
One day though, will my ghost who retreats
to the cobweb on our return, tell you to go
Away as your ghoul fields squarely with me;
they get unrulier each time, leaving

More remnants of that fight we had,
each time, before we leave, because leaving
Is easy and fun, exciting each time,
like snow in the winter, an obvious answer.

But unusual enough for us, each time,
and just enough that we can imitate the dancer
Ghost&Ghoul Co., tap our feet in matching rhythm;
fill in the routine, each time, just barely
To overlook the sink stains and rotting tea leaves,
they make us run, maybe they work with
The ghost and the ghoul, who I can see
behind you, she says come hither.
Eyes wide and wild, seeking my ghost,
I want to answer, scream, stupid stalker
Followed us here, to Holidayland, where we sneak
kisses under the snowy perch
Warm, soft, tender – my ghost imagines
your heart in our hands, retreating sneakily.

Burial

I am preserved under layers of film,
dust, debris and devastation, ladled atop me.

You captured me with a stray hair out of
Place, a belly left hanging loose, a smile dropped.

Dark dawns watch smoke mixing with octopus
tendrils, squeezing, ink, blood, bloody ink into air.

Against this backdrop, I am more of the shadows,
than of the objects I lust for, not tangible but touchable.

In order to contain the fluids of my dusty bottle,
and covering charges for the messes I make,

You reach your hand into me and try to pull out
my lungs, lest they remain dust addled and mirky.

I am a slushy of the disgusting stuff, but at least
I am memorialised, definite, certain, on a path.

If you could really see me now, would you honestly
meet my eyes, I am so hot, clammy, an oyster on boil.

Simmering atop this furnace of broken memories,
my mind has a file of evidence against all who wronged me.

I never forget, even when I want to.
Especially when I want to.

Dates for When Your Sugar Sinks Low

Ma kept a whole box of raisins and dates on your desk,
she reminds you that this is not a joke, that you need to accept
these slimy goodies are going to save you.

You need to breathe back in affirmations the harsh words
you use against your own self, words of wrath and such
displeasure that there was no scope for respite

You were so hard on yourself that you forgot how to live
this life.

It's a balm for the blackouts your anxious soul cause,
the body jitters and seizures where you convulse and capsize
against the firmness of a tender hand placed on your cheek.

Concerned because understanding is far too distant to reach,
a site of total departure where nothing you say
can ever truly convey what you mean,
you eat words.

Because they fill your stomach with substance and
alphabets of gritty, ungodly mirth filled joylessly
a departure.

An arch of the yodelling tree makes you compress
into the seat on your desk,
remember that there is love after all
even when the understanding is too far,
love can cure some and sugar the rest.

Butterfly

Was my childhood a warm cocoon
Of soft and tender memories.

I have always drawn on my arms,
Seeking permanence, watched by wandering adults.
The journey has been a hard one to forget,
To find where my butterfly sits on this arm.

The insects that crawl all over me bother you.

Yet to build their cocoons and morph from the
Chrysalis of unwanted change.

What have I always wanted?

These too will be butterflies on my arm,
Who wants an insect when a possibility is the fluttering thing.
The butterfly is what beauty means to me.

It traces the lines on my arm abandoned
By the grief of my swallowed rage.

For in that metamorphosis,
The thing is a cocoon of skin I shed.

My spine cracking as it unleashes wings
I was meant to fly with.

There is an abandonment in the desert of souls, treat it
The festering lesion
It has marred the skin under my butterfly.

But now there is only the fluttering thing,
It flits all over my arm.
Hiding what it knows I cannot show,
Showing what it knows I cannot hide.

Freudian

It is not my fault I say, multiple times over
Until the louding voice of my scream is
Rendered but a gasp, a whisper of the
Meat we were fighting over cooking
Raw and marinated or tasteless and charred,

You tell me how hard it was to find meat at the supermarket
Where the old lady was fighting for free lemons
How you dodged questions from the prying neighbour
Who peeks into our windows sometimes and smokes
Her cigar with a holder attached, one hand waving
We never acknowledge her, but you like the show.

Like we are a couple on air, who get to display our
disputes for the audience as a running gag, the same
thing almost every time, a raw egg, badly made coffee,
mushy rice, rotting fruit, the smell of smoke in the sheets.

The shopping journey is meditative for you.
Running inventory through your mind,
slapping the papaya to check its freshness,
flipping each egg in the carton to see cracks,
idling in the line as customers count change.

It is coming home that chaos begins to unravel.

The neighbour's smile over our shoulders
whenever we make the mistake of looking over,
plus her occasional appearance to ask for flour
or sugar, among other neighbourly feats

They take a toll on the subtle gadget we are building
Between us, slowly and technically with the
Practised hands of heartbreak and the knowledge
that it is time, to settle into things and slow down
but there is still hope for tonight's dinner.

How to Be Someone Who Cared Less

I was a muddy child, ashy knees and elbows,
round face, bloody braces and glasses
I always had to tape together.
The first time I got into a fight,
the teachers were surprised I had it in me at all,
to not just stand there and take it,
to do something about the incessant
words of horror that every friend I wanted
to call a friend but couldn't, said to me.
In light of what I know now, I think
I was frequently enough not at fault
But I am okay with the knowledge
that I may have been the bad child after all.
The thrower back of punches, with rebuttals
for snide comments on my weight, my acne,
the way I did my hair, the way I laughed, talked, ate,
blew my nose, answered every question in class,
until one day I became this brute of force and fallacious
valour, where my fists could not suffice,
I cried until I could fill rivers of wrongdoings and honestly,
I regret nothing.

If I Set Fire to All That You Hold Dear

Sometimes I play with the things I shouldn't
another kid's toy, the ends of a book borrowed;
sometimes a stomach, bloated, wet and red, working
through digestive medication, to ease the burn.

At the temple gate, I wait for the crowd to clear
Waiting to see if someone like me played with
another's shoes and stole mine this time.
Am I the unforgiving thing, if I eat other's offerings?

I have been scavenging for food and comfort
For as long as I can remember, trying to plug
The parts of me that leak even when I try
My hardest to hide them in black.

I know no hunger, only a craving, a deep
Summoning in my belly and chest that
Needs to be answered, lest I go mad.
Nothing natural in this cycle to binge and purge.

I play with my mind and convince myself
I am not hungry when I am. I am not
Interested in eating out, I am not, I am not.
I play with others and convince them I am happy.

Insolence

My body is my only house
It has four limbs and one head of hair
Did they settle for me as a tenant?

With a scalpel I find new ways to draw lines in my house
Wonderous and labyrinthian, they become secrets
For my walls to whisper about

I am a surgeon, a builder, a home wrecker
I will ruin and rampage what is beautiful
And then when I am disowned.

I will laugh.

Mango Season

You eat the pit of the fruit like a ravenous beast,
fierce pulls and the occasional plop back into the plate
yellowy-orange stains all across your mouth like
a loud slash of the sun burned through you.
you smile, your teeth caked with mango.
Heat prickles the top of my arms like little
soldiers marching to the tune of the tropics, burning
them, roasting them for a feast I am not invited to.
You eat the pit first and then devour the flesh of the
mango from its skin, pulling it off – teeth bared
threatening anyone to take it away from you.
your arms are a mess of juice as it trails down
your elbow and in those moments, you tell me
you wonder if your mother ever truly loved you.
if cutting fruit is a supplement for emotion and
feeding a solution to expressing those feelings
you are sensitive beyond the skin of your body,
while mine bristles under the sun, you are untouched
unknown to the burns and the blisters of the heat.
It is this warmth that you feel inside like an inferno baking
bricks to throw at houses not build them, nothing
about your rage – you say – is purposeful or valuable
you have etched it into the walls of this room many
times over, in different scripts and using different names

but the wonder I hold remains, how you do it, how
with such grace and a total lack of it you tear this fruit
to its pieces and then you wonder if there was ever
truly someone who loved you, if you ever found home in
a person and I, simple-minded as I am, wonder if
the houses you have lived in have not been enough
if home needs to be sought out and torn into a person's
flesh for, if their ribcage does need to expand
to fit in your expressions and silent gestures and
waiting sighs and pained silences, if you need someone
to hold onto when you have these mangoes,
in crates of sun slashed warmth and juice and joy.

Newspaper Elegy

The morning newspaper is an elegy to the job you retired from,
there is an old wound you carry from the field,
it boils and bubbles over once a fortnight

Every morning at 7 it should be here and most days it conforms,
the meek delivery boy smiles chastely at you
as he hands over the newspaper and sighs a relief,

My blistered toe is a testament to your angst
on the one day it doesn't and I have to chase down
the newspaper boy's cycle barefoot, one hand holding my spatula

Work was always so important to you; you were a traveller
of the afflicted kind, wounded and weary from the burdens
you carried but diseased to carry on. Always forward, always
flailing.

Work kept you away and now as you look at me,
I can see you search for the six-year-old that
you bribed with chocolates to hide your daily smokes

I think of that every time I slither in the shadows
to catch my smoke, one hand waving the fumes away,
the other unknotting the same rope around my neck – that
you carried

This grace is ours and meant for eternity, the weight of those
ancestors you always talked about, the treasury of
their honours is checked upon fortnightly

When the wound is obscene, gory, graphic and ghastly,
it shuns possibilities of gentle departure,
yours was not, like the wound and the treasury

Leaving was not easy for you, detaching your sensibility,
for uncertainty - retirement, at this site a gas bubble emerged
masking your anger in the patchoulis of putrid fragrance.

Now that newspaper is an anchor, drowning us,
weighing more than any hopes we carried
for what walking away a final time would be like.

That travel never came and the rest was vanquished
sentimental and slumping. It gave up before you ever
truly tried and now maybe you look back to the headlines

Those newspapers carry and lament on the past
so long not forgotten, it shakes the ground beneath our house
and hostility brews in the kitchen alongside tea

That newspaper is an elegy from the job you retired from,
sliding out of the folds between those words rest assurances
I cannot give you and the stagnation you cannot accept.

Showmanship

There is a knife twirling under my nails.
I could pull away, if I wanted to though.
It stays twirling, collecting the soot of my skin
And the tissue under it
I shouldn't scream, that's impolite, dirty.

I knew,
knew better,
knew sooner,
knew for me
and for others,
That knives draw blood and yet
I played.
Happy, smiling, twirling my hair to the rhythm of the knife,
And it drew blood.

But I liked this one, the handle, something about the point
it made in class.
Bent on my nails, it peels back
And drops my nail like rancid mass
Wilting on an ancient academic carpet

Am I screaming now? I am displeased,
Pleased, please, please, please, please.
I held the knife and comforted its excesses,

Booing off all others' scars and scrapes
Telling anyone who would listen that this knife
unlike all the others, it did not stab.

Look, stainless steel and all. Not like
The other knives, he did not need salvation.

But then I had to leave, hands folded
Sheepish, quiet and ashamed,
About giving up, walking away with my proverbial tail between my legs.
Even as I watch my nail rot on that same carpet,
I am bound to repeat, not all knives are bad,
some only slice red apples.

Wonderment

You sneeze with your whole body
Thrice in succession, face wrinkled
With years of use, wear and tear
I freeze, every time, as it rings out

My wince is noticeable and you
Straighten, you don't even need
Words to hit me as hard your
Fists, this pitch hurts my throat

And each time, I am left with such
a vast and unkind longing that I am
ashamed of my own desires, not
knowing the language of my wounds.

You forgot to teach it to me, maybe
For a job, or maybe because if I am
As colonised as you claim, that too
Is your doing, I have no other words.

My tongue is swollen and bruised for
Every other vocabulary that is not this,
But using this evokes your suspicions,
You are a good servant, you tell me.

Learning the tongue of the masters,
but they left you with this language
first, before I was even here or there.
Sadly, I am bound to make the excuses I do.

The Garden Is a Full Sentence

I almost came here as a complete thing
in this garden of mongoose,
I came the lonely viper.
Venom dripping poison I lather myself,
scrubbing and washing away what is in me.
The mongooses, they stare at me.
A threat – already made.
I hiss back assurances of peace,
But my fangs shine bright and
my scales are glowing.
My dance of joy around the garden
looking up to the flowers high and low,
sees each mongoose step away.
So, I slither closer, arms stretched wide
welcoming them.
Only, I came as a viper today
and I have no arms
A mongoose growls and
I have no choice but to slither away
For I am as double skinned as they come,
Duplicitous, hide-changing, backtracking fraud
It is only today that they are able
to see the venom drip down my teeth

But another day, every other day,
my teeth will go on rotting,
my smile flexing only brighter.
All fake, all ghastly, all loathing
like the viper among the mongoose.

Pickling

Salt, chilli, oil, mango
Salt for the wounding,
to bleach and leech of blood and water.
Chilli for the tears, for the raw burn under my tongue,
to boil and heat this sack of organs.
Oil for viscosity, it floats and mixes,
sloshes and slurs, mustard even for the fever.
Mango for the time, summer – always summer, falling on tin sheds.
And there between these I sit and watch you do magic.
Pickling, I stop and look out the window lest I feel too much
And the salt if not enough, my eyes can provide
I have bent.
With you over the mangoes, mixing,
hands digging through the sludge and syrup of chilli and oil
The memory of a stray cut resurfaces as the chilli pierces my skin
And my salt unravels from my eyes,
tumbling in soft turrets as you go on mixing
Pickling mangoes, preserving them for the days to come
The salt is like silence, it improves longevity
Like practice in pickling,
this salty silence is measured in potency
Too little and the mangoes rot
Too much and they are inedible

Planning a Surprise Birthday Party With Moderation

You brush the sticky crumbs of my birthday cake
from between your fingers, hands like waves
dancing in the moonlight.
Just as this night is, I felt perfect, happy, content, swollen
just right.

That same moonlight, streams through strewn cups and shines
On the cracks of that one plate, we broke as we tried to shift
The leftover cake.
I am glad your interjection waited the course
Of our night.

All low calorie.
I know I need to watch the scale, you tell me it is essential.
That my jeans get looser and breasts tighter, and I would be
Perfect.

As the night concluded, and we bid everyone off,
You told me, this effort that you made for me.
And now the cake and the wine, and the food
All claw to exit my stomach and out my mouth.

Would that please you?

I am a burly husk of a person, loose and soft and strong,
Silent and angry because all of me is measured
Down to the grams of my breath, and the crumbs
On my shirt, I am counted until I am just a number.

So, when you go to bed tonight,
I will take a walk to the corner shop, buy a cigarette
And a sandwich, eating over my full stomach,
Contemplating how small I would be to walk away from you.

Turgidity in the Heart

This heart grows outside my body
I dream every night that it has grown
Into a wolf, howling at the moon and
At the strange men that pass by me

I worry that I am looked at every time
I step outside the house, feverish and
Spotted, red and blotchy, out of breath,
Is it my whole face and not just a spot?

Walking around, I often forget just how
Much space the width of my body takes
Knocking people's shoulders, grazes of
A man's arms on my back, frequently a pat

In my dream my heart grows so big,
it squelches salty blood outside my
body and splatters on my mother's
pristine carpet, evidence of the space I took.

After that, I curl up and sleep
On top of the stain, but
Somehow it is bigger than me
And now I know, it cannot be hidden.

Villainy

You find me in the moments I steal from others,
Little dregs of the day, gargantuan days that feed
The soul of damned and demented just like you

My body is a shared location, it houses more than
I am comfortable with sharing, in measured parts
I chalk out the lines of me I can bear to part with

The stolen essence of my days is a retreat for my
Body to breathe as loudly as it pleases and exhale
The fumes of others' sorrows into the winds of yore

You take my hand even though I lined it just for me
In this moment, a chalk outline for the martyred
relic I have rewarded my family with, and you

Who I save no manners for, get the dirty grimy
Aftermath of the crime scene, a site where the
Evidence has been bagged, all else left to rot.

I am the remnants of perusal, lifted up, flipped
Around, made to dance a jig, and rig the system
Of organisation my organs had previously known
All in the name of some desperate selfish respite.

Lily of the Valley: Part One

I married the monkey king and I do not regret it
I was the sky and the stars, I was Tara, one of five
Eternally revered, before and after my time.

When we wed, my husband told me that he
was a monster of the finest making, all brawn,
tempering against earth, wind and water.

We were happy. I was a happy wife and a happy
woman, pious and flawed in the ways we women
secretly are. I was content without changing him.

He fought, and how, so valiant, a true born leader.
He would laugh to me, Tara, I am the monkey king
because I climbed my way to the very top.

When he returned from his battles, all sodden
blood and dirt, I would wash him, and he would
wash his eyes for the sins they saw committed.

We had a life, well lived, and a son I was happy
To raise, while his father went and waged wars
On those who dared that he do so.

I lined my lips with his half-eaten grapes,

Kohl for my eyes from the ashes of his enemies,
and then I would watch, as a peace ballooned, intolerable.

When we were young, and my husband was just mine,
he would tell me that this life was not his choice,
but destined. And today, surrounded by our trees, I cried.

He said he wanted to be a poet, or painter,
to colour me into the stars, night sky in audience
and watch them twinkle their applause.

When he was gone, I often revisited our beginnings.
Simpler because life was harder on us, until
we became the whetstone, judge, jury and executioner.

He would leave me in the forest of discarded
stones and jewels, where he made me a hut
I lived with the genteel warmth of a true monkey queen.

I would not give up the luxuries of the new life
we created, and my name, the name I was given
On the day we wed, it was me and I was a star.

Lily of the Valley: Part Two

My husband's brother was an unkind man.
I was virtuous, my husband was brave, my son
was innocent and he was ambitious.

It flooded through his veins, pumping his
chest, splitting the hair off his back, until
He saw nothing between him and the crown.

A man more pious than me, offered to help
My brother-in-law, if he helped him in return.
I will burn your bridge, if you build mine.

And then he shot my husband, I do not know how
Or where it happened, but that the women of
My chambers surrounded me in preparation.

I shook off my ornaments, they no longer had
a place on my body, and I no longer had a place
in the palace. My monkey king was gone.

His brother lusted for me, and I knew he did.
His eyes ate away at me until I was nothing
But a bone for him to gnaw on.

When he told me about his brother, my husband,

I was ready, with my son held tightly against
my chest, warding myself from that gaze.

But he snatched my son, promising to raise him
As his father would have. And I was just as
Voiceless then as I have been virtuous always.

I retreated, childless and widowed, to the trees
my husband wooed me under, he would swing
on them with his barrel-like arms and make me laugh.

And when this usurper returned from that war,
my son had grown into a monkey prince I did not
recognise, or wish to embrace, but he touched my feet.

A righteous king went looking for his wife
and I waited for the last thing my husband left,
a son I had not fed at my breast, he grew untested.

My son had dishonoured me, dishonoured the
decency of enmity, we were the monkey kingdom
and even our foes were met with dignity.

But this heathen, raised by his hedonistic uncle,
husband murderer that he was, had been dishonourable.
Cursed by the louding echo of wronged women.

He bent before me, bless me mother, and I flinched,
I could smell the villainy of the usurper on his shoulders,

and my body wretched at the thought of his deeds.

Then came the men, fellow warriors of my
husband's monkey clan, laughing about how
my son had disrobed the fallen queen.

My soldiers, mine now, went regardless of my blessing,
and they returned cheery, while I was a burning ball of
poison. Hoping to one day burst like the stars.

They laughed and they laughed, until their bellies
filled with glee, and I sat under the tree, wondering
would their laughter find meaning if my husband were king.

I watched the aftermath in my kingdom, rightfully mine
snatched from my beloved, and me. I broke under deadly
sounds of a war I refused to vote for. Offering only silence.

Instagram Haiku

Five thirty pm
One shoe missing the other
Locked in library

Letting

My need for approval, is
maintenance paid, quarterly to you.
Emerging from a cloud, humid, I
Watch you flounder, hands tied
And for the first time.
I salivate, thinking, that I too
Could fix your bind with my words,
Encouraging and sparingly un-gentle.

I asked for a buoy, or a jacket,
Or even those floaties, I wore
When you first taught me how to swim.
Nothing.

But passing time has reversed our positions,
I am unbound, the water is kinder to me
And I can float, or swim against the tides.
Your bones are no longer on your side.
And I do worry if I struck that pot too
In the genetic lottery.

Emotion is all around us and I have little
Forgiveness in me, I learnt to stay afloat
After drowning plenty and choking through
Salt and muck and algae, all to see if you

Were ever looking at me, just looking.

I could walk away, I have found land
And I am Prospero, this knowledge
Would be victory enough for me.
Not knowing if you floated back up
Or not, absolves me of duty, I hope.

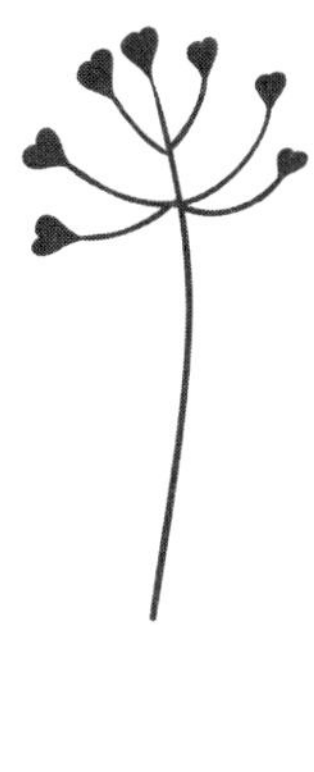

In the Event I Do Make It Out

In case this message finds you too late,
we will meet again in some kirana shop,
where you are haggling over rice puffs
and I am pulling on the end of your shirt
take me home, I don't want to be outside.

I forgot to say goodbye, because I am
Admittedly quite ill-mannered and you
did your very best Ma, but I was made
of stranger stuff, not sterner though
you tried there too; I was belligerent.

A fool, who just wanted to eat cake
And not bread, who wanted the
Freedom of breathing bigly and exhaling
In short sharp puffs; slimy and slipping
Through the years spent teaching me etiquette.

I can't say I ever hated you, but I don't
think we'd get along if I was not a piece
of you. I was so alike you, strong-headed
and unyielding, but my branches began
to shatter against your winds, Ma.

Make the most of the cherries in the yard
And bake them into little treats. Rewards.
One for washing the dishes, one for sorting
my bed, one for the weights I lifted, another
for all the times I cut just enough to stop.

Do not remember me like the crushed bug
Between your palms, remember me uncrushed,
Unencumbered, maladaptive and malicious.
Buzzing in the air around you, judging you
From my urn on the mantle, eyes rolling at
The beautiful shrine you have made, to lords
And me, I have joined them now, in my grace.

Lorekeeping and the Dermal Druids

Bigness that engulfs me, oh Amma,
beneath these layers, on three whole days
I go without, shelling out inches of skin.
It's on sale, take it, before I abscond,
culprit in the making. I wish, with more
than my lungs, someone would display us
With tender love and care. Gently,
picking one by one shards of glass, stuck,
plucking on morsels of skin that burn.

Ma, there is something that runs
lines all over my body, across my shoulders
and down my arms there are old ones of silver,
Angry red ones, harsher duller purples,
some no bigger than a sliver.
Others slash across my stomach,
weed thrasher in the thicket; slowly
they unravel like whorls over my chest,
wildly, wavy, they slither, whispering fire,
splaying poison in your lore of words untethered.

Ma, Amma, Ma, mine of the skin and blood
we share and the hearts we don't, forsaken

in channels of clogged oil, ignite me with ether
and watch as it departs, detaching from
the soul of our skins, blue scarred orange, yours glowing.
Envelop my skin and soul,
basket it within the visions burning my surface
To be yours unlike me; this skin,
tape it back together, removing the heart that hangs
from my ribcage for your love and its tightening embrace.

Hold the skin of my hand M,
gently between your palms,
Sit with me, on that chair of grief,
we made it with the dust
We shed, we mixed it into poisons,
skilled mirrors and organic halves
of rotten skin lathered in love,
only love, only concerned love, never lust.

Lust less is skin like this, only nasty, only hostile,
bitter, biting, butchered love but not caring
Love, only love charged with crimes, of theft,
in bargained scars, buy with sparing.

Amma, speak to me like you speak to my skin,
These layers of dust dulled beige,
they're stretched too thin.
Amma, lather my words, my voice
with the same malai cream,
cover my skin with haldi, I am turned, forever;

but that yellow will not redeem the villainy
soiling my heart, sodden thuds have muddied it the same.

my skin, peel it back, muscle, tissue, fibre;
somewhere on the bone, you'll see my name.

Amma this skin has stretched beyond
to keep holding me in an organ-less body.
Bloated from the salt of life, haltingly
The unravelled seat of my voice is gathered,
and sewn into the folds of our skin,
yours and mine that sagged on bone,
fleetingly in silence, I disowned
this skin for it has burned me;
and as you weep, there rest a few
more bubbles of rage, knifed in deep.

If We Just Lay Here

If we just lay here,
measured in minutes or miles
waiting in the shadows
of our own forgotten selves.
The casuarina tree finds me
buried under its veins.
Throbbing and drenched
in the sap of a wound
that refuses to close.
There is no relief or finesse in
Our hearts for the mistakes
we made before we decided
to lie down.
Is there any kind of pardon
meant for the likes of us,
Can the lightning that
struck two inches to my left
Hit me instead and I will sublimate, willingly.

Monsoons

This forest that surrounds my home
is the realest thing to me.
My legs scarred from the years I spent learning how to climb them
The skirt I wore in all those endeavours
still flares around my body
Waiting for the lithe spring of a tree
to brush past it in earnest.
In those moments where the sun meets the edges of the tree's crown, I am smitten by the colour that the sky can hold
For I am but a tiny human and the sky is this canvas I have imposed into being happy
that this doorway to the heavens is riddled with a myriad clouds,
some bunny-shaped
some popsicle-shaped
And I can taste it on my tongue, the fluff, the weather of oranges
That dripped down my chin
and left sticky residue on my fingers.
There is an expression in my mother's mother tongue
for someone who is gently foolish,
a fool who could mean no harm to anyone even if they willed it
and that word pops into my head
like the zing of zesty citrus popsicles,
the blades of the grass tickling my back.

From my vantage point so far beneath
the sky and the clouds and the tree
an ant of the larger kind, four-limbed
and musty-smelling like the smell
of calla lilies blooming
at the cusp of monsoon,
fresh perfumed air against
the saccharine joy
of wandering up far too high
and biting into the fruit
and the leaf and the tree
branch and the ant,
just to feel them burst against my tongue
to give texture to my soul
and substance to my gut,
there is a bespoke charm
to the tree above me,
looming like a giant
laughing at my baby being,
creaking
against the winds of the southwest
Corner, just waving its leaves,
dancing
to a song I must strain my ears to hear
and yet I am but this person
admiring a tree,
waiting patiently
for an eye to open
and acknowledge my devotion.

Midnight Coffee

The coffee sits under the window,
Wisps of steam slither out,
reaching the hanging frames
Of frozen time and when
the steam meets the icy glass it sizzles.
But the commotion is not enough to wake you
Your coffee waits by the window
Where I have left it, walking away,
at distance from the effervescing foam of a coffee
You will not drink
I know
I know
I know
And yet, every night when you ask for a cup of coffee
It's there,
Under the window
Wisps of steam wading the dusky air of this night,
the previous and the next.

The Room Where It All Happens

At home I have five eyes and two mouths,
One for the fruit Amma cut and the other to talk
The room is wallpapered and old,
Its flowers looking fondly at generations of fruit eaters
There is a huge water mark that last year's
Monsoon
Left
On the wall, it stung, the glue fading into purple
And the wall, still there, watches my descent
Into this madness of saccharine joys,
with my many eyes,
the flowers dance for them
in sugary swings of sweet nothings
Not for me, I am mundane to it,
but my eyes, they are new
They went to college
Away
Leaving
The flowers, and souring fruit behind.
Amma says she doesn't wait, but the flowers
have another tale to tell that
Tightens,
Leaves

and then returns in the placations of the fruit,
Mango for your grades,
A pear for your heart,
These apples for your silenced tongue.

Snake Apparitions

I want to shed my skin like snakes, all
alone, ridding myself of an address,
I no longer wish to call home.

Deciduous in temperament and unwilling
To accept any help. Especially yours.
I want to be rid of this body, so
Just in case someone else, like you
Cannot convince me, that I say things I
Know I never said.

But I believed you the last time
I was accused, there's just so many
Words that I utter between hisses.

I believed you, hazy eyed and fumed high
On bath salts, so inebriated in the joy
Your presence brought me,
That I drank poison from my own fangs,
Thinking it was wine.

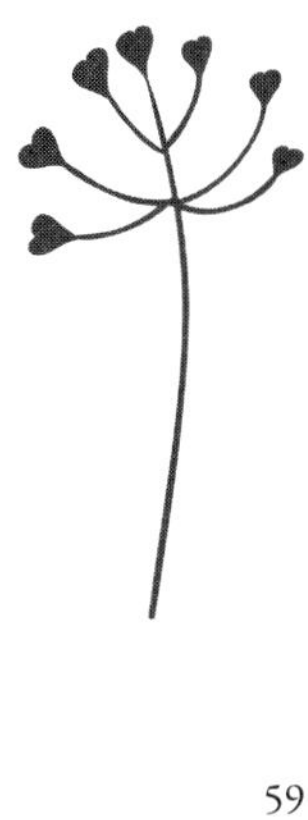

Acknowledgements

Vikas Rakheja and Bidisha Srivastava are incredible publishers, editors and advocates for my work. Without their vision and support, much of this collection would have failed to blossom. The team at Manjul Publishing House and Amaryllis has been great, their support and faith in my work means the world to me. Thanks to each and every one of you for giving my work a chance.

I would like to thank Ila Manish, Avishi Srivastava, Maseera Khan, Kuhoo Singh and Shireen Kalra. I am eternally grateful for your existence in my life.

Ila, you are an actual angel who has read the many, many drafts of my work. I would be nowhere without you. Avishi saw me writing the very beginnings of this collection. Her absolute commitment to the belief that one day my work would see the light of day kept me going in the times of most confusion. Maseera and Kuhoo, you have read my work from when it was scribblings on the corners of my maths notebook and always believed that I would make it something real. Thank you for the undying belief. And to Shireen, who understood my need to write like no one else, thank you.

I would like to thank my teachers and professors, who have helped me reach this path in life. I would like to extend my deepest gratitude to Professor Arunava Sinha, who has always been a champion of my work and given me the best feedback I could ever get. I would like to thank Professor Arpita Das and Professor Janice Pariat for their support, feedback and vital teachings about the writing craft. I am also grateful for Professor Sumana Roy, whose advice on poetry and the poetic enriched my understanding of the craft and helped me become a sharper editor of my own work.

Lastly, and most crucially, I would like to thank my family. My sister, thank you for your brain and your kind heart, I am eternally indebted to both of them. To my parents, who have been bastions of support and have always heard me out in my moments of despair. Ma, you are the bravest and strongest person I know, thank you for teaching me the value of sheer hard work and dusting my knees whenever I fell. Papa, you have the eyes of an eagle and your editorship of my work has only made it so much better; thank you for picking the best soybeans always. Ma and papa, thank you so much for making me the person I am today. It was all of your support and your acceptance of my need to hide in corners with books, letting me run my imagination wild – even when it got me trouble with the stories I wrote or told and ultimately sitting me down to tell me that writing was valid, it was good enough and that I could do it – that drives me on the best and worst days. I will be eternally grateful for the three of you.